Views of the Hudson

Also by Angela Gardner:

Poetry

Parts of Speech (2007)

twelve labours (2009)

The Night Ladder (2009)

ANGELA GARDNER

Views of the Hudson

— A New York Book of Psalms —

Shearsman Books
Exeter

First published in the United Kingdom in 2009 by
Shearsman Books Ltd
58 Velwell Road
Exeter EX4 4LD

www.shearsman.com

ISBN 978-1-84861-080-4
First edition

Acknowledgements:

The author gratefully acknowledges the award of a Churchill Fellowship
that enabled her to travel to New York during the writing of this poem.
Thanks also to Laurie Duggan, Ian Friend and Kerry Kilner who took the
time to read and comment on the manuscript during its development.

Some of the phrases in italics are
freely quoted: in the valley of salt [8], God is our God [12 &13], some
days I dig a pit [15], the king of all the earth [25], . . . our houses will
continue forever [34], the nights are long [41], sword raised over the
head [43] are from The Psalms, King James version; neon in daylight [24]
from 'A Step Away From Them' by Frank O'Hara; scritti di storia dell'arte
[44] first publication of the Florentine technique of fresco conservation.

Nb: the poems are sonnets in that I count them as 14 lines,
i.e I count the gaps as lines also.

Cover: Digital image taken from panels four and five of the nine-panel
monoprint *Vertical Coast* by Angela Gardner, 2006. First shown Redcliffe
City Art Gallery, Queensland, and copyright © Angela Gardner, 2006.

For my parents

VIEWS OF THE HUDSON

1

the world turns from us
not from our feelings
(though everyone's heart leaks)

in the aeroplane
in pools of light
screens flutter mutely
but tell me nothing
not even that one small choice
they made

an announcement warns
take care
contents may shift during flight

2

the day I arrived—eye to the lens
the authority of the camera
which cannot lie. Unbelieving scanners
held like a hand of safety from the clouds
ungloved, lace cuffed, slim wrested
How could we ever doubt
their almost sequin encrusted weaponry?
(biometrically matched to our photographs
eyes open and clearly visible)
The reassembled image or thunder
authenticated as the voice from above
I imagine on the wall behind his head
three budgie wings in flying formation
. . . a world created by angels

3

under this sky here is perfection
A god that surrounds himself with
thieves adulterers advocates
godly and ungodly all demanding
I am here

And me? Why are these two lives
in place at once?

Why do they stand so far apart?

In the crowded terminal at JFK
I can hear the uncomfortable silence
in all this noise

4

1954 or 1967? it only makes a difference
in density. Passers-by avoid eye contact
or each other or themselves
Even reflections in glass provoke this
so why stand in their sway?
(an unlikely exhortation)
Blow through these streets
clothes as barely in contact with bodies
as our thoughts—after all day and night
screens blaze without us

Stop the car you tell me
:I have totally missed the point or will
violence is inevitable—not sleep

5

I stand in awe
the sheer volume of it sheer

or below have I misunderstood?
As if for blessing
there are broken filaments of dusk or dawn
a voice at day that leans over my shoulder:
more light to straighten the path
remove the cheats and night workers
drive flatterers' tongues back to their beds
in their mouths How to stay?
walk don't walk
it's not always a choice
or even so clear, come the light of day

6

... clear and daylit
and tipped into a promised land
of refrigerators, aircon, long wheelbase cars
A pile em high sell em cheap arcadia
hardly incremental of utopian amendments
This is what I dreamed of
Spanish American & Mexican food served
it was what we were looking for yes?
Our rightful inheritance of home ... of home
the lie of the land (flattened and regularised)

Even in the eye of the beholder
everything to hand and something
for others to envy

7

a little black dress
a box cut red jacket with overlong sleeves
a full length coat, a skirt
a purple shirt with a cuff full of buttons

that's my jacket
you keep your two eyes on it

two figures caught against a lighted wall
searching the fine tonality of skin

we struggle with nakedness
from cleavage to cunt

8

in the valley of salt
where I am high as a kite one minute
and lost the next. Turn to look again
he returns unravaged. Basquiat arms raised
above his tarnished gargantuan head
Gold-perfumed and irresistible
pins around his waist
so photorealistically human
(for so we envy and aspire)

With him at my side
there is a strange elasticity to reality
each object in heightened conversation
with emptiness

9

A voice divides space
days surrounded by strangers
(not even enemies)

I am a child again
waiting—maybe to be picked up
or walk away suffuse
days I wake alone bereft
Above our heads (doll and child)
is the skyline of someone talking
and someone maybe listening, maybe not
fire escapes stop above our heads
metal cellar doors open below our feet
I try to wake to understand another day

10

what's with the vanity?
Don't ask what the photos say
(it's not spot the difference
as owners of this real estate suggest)
A strait-jacket squat amongst it
will give me everything (only theirs to give)

Listen if early flying machines stayed up
even just briefly, it was through love and string
and anyone can buy string
even at two a.m. there is string to be had
this is your inheritance
quit weeping and put your trust in it
anyone can buy string

11

The sidewalks are full of tulips to admire
to buy. Tulips bowed under the weight
of their colour
burnt orange, cadmium red, Bordeaux
a broken line along parrot lips
& tongue
I've taken note of the oppressive scale
of the clocks on the mantelpiece
hurrying that obscures the face of beatitude
I avoid scurrying
but only just. Below the apartment
is the regularised grammar of the streets
an architect's model
. . . the unstoppable city

12

this is *the* place and everyone knows it
and I am here (do you detect triumphalism?)
Almost unfurled—center the city here
here where I stand and the city doesn't stop!

The city trails grey sky from freeways
and tunnel mouths beside the Hudson
But mark well the towering architecture
the elevators and escalators of Macy's
And as you walk the streets
consider the question of scale
the harmonious regularity of the grid

God is our God

13

Is this what the city thinks? *God is our God—*
Behold the avenues!
Over a week here now
and where is there ever redundant light
or movement?
A man plays music on a street corner
and we move past something priceless
or its facsimile
Is it possible to mistake one for the other
outside a storefront at night?
We keep walking as he plays
All these people and no-one able
to spare me a dime
          hear me set me free

14

My own grimed reflection
shades of mortality rubbed and dissolved
to a hieroglyphic snail of meaning
over and over
over and over
in each storefront window

Instead here is something else—a wooden box
with drawers full of powder colour
and a fire that is curiously in tatters
Look! you asked so little and still I desire
bright armour, the top of an unexpected hill

. . . I look for Grace

15

and if I find it
. . . it will be at the point
where the mirror or blurred window
or the book I carry
are where I would be
downtown
between marble entrance foyer and something tinsel
a doorman building at Christmas maybe
If a book
then bookshelves are pulled from the rubble
and missing pages prevent cave-ins

some days I dig a pit
to fall straight in!

16

like a fool
hung around the neck of Fifth Avenue
nothing happens (which we know is impossible:
there should be a battered truck
or the first chocolate ice of summer)
Instead there is shopping and crowds
something for everyone
everyone for something

Men in evening dress look at women
perched
on tiny chairs covered in expensive fabric
Maybe I'll make something of it
tomorrow . . .

17

my shoes pinch at these new streets
and another day's high tide
of litter hits the sidewalks
and leaves the city exhausted
Emptiness, fullness what's the difference?
Fuck beauty!
I'm one collective noun too many
If I thought it was all about me . . .

Two dogs race past after a frisbee

On expert advice
I have misplaced the experience of reality

tears stream down my face

18

clouds reach towards the sun
in a spectacular act of perspective
hiding within my own shadow

Sometimes I am fearless in this city!

She could draw lines across the sky
though she has surprisingly little to say
of the past (how long is forever to hide?)
sits mute before forgotten political posters
pasted over with advertising

On the sidewalk metal filing cabinets
are removed from a building

19

. . . I trust in silence
as we walk under trees
Bryant Park *unter den Linden*
on crushed gravel paths (so very European
a place where cities have already
been made and destroyed
or just buried under indifference)
. . . a hand outstretched
The city is being documented by amateur
photographers—open lens intent
the workers united will never be defeated

and we shall find a new refuge
for the oppressed . . .

20

a crowd gathers around
the people with the microphones

The Workers United will Never be Defeated

Spanish American & Mexican

it was what we were looking for yes?
home . . .
the lie of the land (flattened and regularised)
I stand back
(so carefully constructed I find nothing to say)

for us the projects are sketchy at night past 10th

21

Us oppressed?
Two women avoid seeing the beggars
form identical wry expressions

a child asks: Are we going to China?
No honey just Chinatown
                              It's a very long busride
It's on Manhattan island
we won't get lost

Mothers know a missing hand a difficult bower
their own excellence in irony and self deceit
Out of the mouths of babes—
out of their mouths under our feet

22

this weekend morning
the whole island is lined up in skyscrapers
the NY Times towers paper and ink
Letters of light are back projected
in all December's lighted windows
Out of their mouths but over our heads
looking out, looking away
looking at nothing
I remind myself—looking at nothing is important
Greed—a whispered voice—the magic show
could that be authentic even when cutesy?
Children pose as Christmas toys
Even as one child sings
twinkle twinkle ickle star

23

I take my place surging with the crowd
the apple is back in fashion
and all of this is mine   for now
to recline in the dark on battered leather seats
The Hudson is forlorn in the rain
its Oyster Bars open but empty

None of the films rate many stars or box-office
and there's an unlikely ice-storm as a plot device
Onscreen the sun is a tisane
weak wintry delicate
that refuses to stay in my head
We slip into the already neon
the substitute night reflecting on the water

24

Walking under epileptic street signs
neon in daylight
beauty and stupidity

I forget celebrity is always mass produced
and still looks like cheap plastic toys
we crowd around insistent expectant
needlessly amazed

At night I slip and fall darkness under me

No! it can't be like this
I continue to do as I should
. . . so why won't it work anymore?

25

this is where it is all happening
hedge funds, share options, arbitrage
the accumulation
and dissipation of inheritance
the wash of its tide in and out
Ordinary men that we crowd against
fat and rumpled and harried like us

Say money is the god of us all
whether you have it or not
acknowledge it

the king of all the earth

26

here in this crowded space
dripped paint on polished concrete
an old-fashioned sink and stuff on the floor
stuff
Over us a narcotic flinch of music
that makes me anxious

I want to believe it makes a difference
our crowding together like this
pooling our burden of neurological disaster
into the other side of a dream

as if a voice will say . . .
Quiet . . . quiet on set

27

that voice . . . listen
(is it a good voice or a bad voice?)

the things I see and hear
over the noise of the trains
the white noise of the day
Figures trawl through threadbare clothes
a ruff of feathers perched on skinny shoulders
repeat after the ad break
everything that went before
repeat

after the ad break neutral expression
ask yourself *Would you trust this man?*

28

but who to trust
a face disfigured by music?
Bent over overstuffed furniture
it is so unseemly so undercooked
even the portraits look down
on my casual rates
There is someone trapped in a corner
but serves him right as he is paid
to research the future of cooking shows
The guests circle or pace like animals
captive he attempts to offer canapés
(fat is flavour!)

but they insist on 98% fat-free

29

Some buildings tower over our lives
become our architecture of existence

the days remain unquiet
with the inequality of money
narrow passageways of loss or opportunity
Subdued in this metal box
a daily commute ends
an overwhelming vertical ascent
    — not contemplative and slow
but fearful and enclosed

and with all the city below my feet
I am at my closest to prayer

30

I wait
struggle against owning this life
the slowness of flesh
honest work the honest day
everything in danger of a tidy mind

mortgage a fifty minute hour of therapy
for a book *Teach Yourself Tango*
All the steps of pride and loneliness
in diagrams for ease of use
Practice Makes Perfect!

and after all where else would I go for abuse
without you?

31

Don't look down into a day
that has no understanding
of what is won or lost
Terrified by the height (32nd floor)
distorted flat to optical illusion

all of this . . .

Stand up soon as maybe:
the hopelessly young (it can be)
the unprepared to express an idea
or build a world
no standing on airport roadways
no exceptions

32

During daylight we talked
but now we fingerpoint on top of the world
& with the light fading
we believe at last we know

I stand next to Superman
an icarus figure on a downward trajectory
he wears wraparound aviator sunglasses
and is surprisingly flatchested
Not super hero, I decide, but winged
& contemplating heaven from on top of a building
I haven't decided and maybe neither has he
upright and innocent
he could be just plain out of it

33

NYPD stands taut behind him
Courtesy Professionalism Respect

I am one of them—the fallen
fearful of abandonment
no abandoh me

. . . and birds will fall from the sky

Later unconvinced
I carefully remove my shoes
as suicides often do
while my clothes stand up
encamped around my body

34

and the obituaries—what do they do?
Or all the guns (or just one of them)
the hopeful face of youth shown dead
the killer in a more recent photo
older now
Upstate in a bare winter
both begin and end in time
the trees may just be monochrome
ink stained after a spectacular Fall

Understand: all of us
we carry nothing away we rot

but act as if our houses will continue forever

35

Though there are noticeable points
of pressure or mental illness
and voice recognition software
here is perfection loud noise
and litigants
the flat decorative faux radiance
a placard of lies
Everything coexists here
if you can cope this is the place to be
millions know this.

Despite the odds
I now cite the discovery of the mute control
as an attainable goal

36

gauze the perfect gaze blurry
in forbidden happiness
At eye level on the bathroom floor
posture entwined with flowers
(. . . maybe I could wear floral shirts)
Ideas look more noticeable:
the maximum load capacity
of this room is 3000
My right hand I marvel at it
against the uniformity of white tiling
nothing there, nothing troubling
just stars circling my head

Prone I chase hapless

37

Now the cold has set in
I judge myself hardly
a forgotten face in the crowd
Hardly a forgotten face
in the crowd

My hand previously marvellous
refuses to obey
while my heart is removed
and left tilted
    —   it is a bird on a chain
looking down on the city

I cannot fly — hold me

38

Beware those around you
they have dirty hands and a slippage of values
Words in my mouth coincide with rituals
with paranoia. *plastic overshoes*
At the moment emptiness
is just that.

The cab streams calibrations
of emptiness and paranoia
an unfortunate compromise *exquisitely*
to a blurred and abstracted sidewalk
the past is obliterated as soon as I pass

emptiness is just emptiness

39

But emptiness as idea:
remember the double feature?
Afternoon's celluloid escape
into the safe suspended warmth of belief?

The baddie always in a black hat
getting it in spades. The promise of retribution
and sins punished by the final reel
Up against John Wayne it really was no contest
Extras appear from the top of a cliff
an army of repeats (digitally enhanced or real?)

If I lie down unable to get up
another will take my place

40

an enigmatic look into the camera
from his corroded yet blissful face
captured on film as he poses ecstatically
before a mirror

How do the sensitive faces of men
relate to music?

One indolently held foot can make me believe
it's too late we can't go back
the sea is hard against the wall
and we are captive of our beliefs

Head-on until the final note
and who would know what that was like?

41

A man under advertising banners
removes what is left of millibars of pressure
from well-stocked shelves
They were imported from distant islands
with worthless currency
as weather
the unconscious hears overhead
unable to sleep
while germs walk like cattle over the skin

the nights are long
make haste to help me

sweat rains the atmosphere

42

all such discards *open the dark*
and we rehearse their lines
(a far cry)
There are conflicts where everyone escapes
in the same direction
What's the cross-street?
while those left behind huddle in makeshift tents
(that laconic shelter left by incidental action)

He leans in a doorway almost stylised
a full length photorealist portrait
followed by laughter
It is difficult to recognise
what others see as degeneracy

43

Another substitute night
shines from the scans—it appears
minor parts of the body have taken control
become unnecessary organs of growth
It is all so . . . *sword raised over the head*
Who said illness really is the perfect gift?

At the Art Gallery
waiting for visiting hours
contrast Rothko's build of glazes—all is serene
even on the reverse all the children in safety glasses
say 'Look! This is Science' (deliberately capitalized)
its awkward camouflage of narcotics

44

I go visit in the land of the dead
I can describe it perfectly:
cut out figures in front of a cream sofa
and at heart a history of money
able to advance over all obstacles

The man in a doorway
has the face of a smoker
a rumpled book-filled head *devouring words*
Another beside him stares intently
making a double portrait with American flag

The Fall brings monsters into being
scritti di storia dell'arte

45

newly gone I can't believe them dead
all transgressions forgiven
bones clay-fired and gritty
grainy photographs of stacked cardboard boxes
each numbered and stored

a horse-drawn tram
takes puzzling relativity away
and there is silence apart from
two competing sidewalk televisions

Above my head
light streams from out of its box
and the horse walks free from its traces

46

... I stay until night closes in
and squalour darkens the palette

the metal deck singing

a woman crouches abed
with generations of her lovers
Above her head a drypoint old man lusts
over a naked young woman
who'll bring him down, their mouths their lips
By morning
her lover is a lamb curled at the end of the bed

... we buy sell trade and finance

47

I am unashamed
What am I bid
?

       for an all singing all dancing emptiness
the clouded triptych of an old woman's face

nobody likes those sort of girls
crowded by surface decoration
and their transgressive tobacco leaf, chocolate,
sugarcane sweetened breath
their teeth-bitten pierced tattooed bodies
I look — pretending
what on earth could they teach me?

48

so many channels of loss or opportunity
(hide your face)

watching soft porn—nights making love

What is she doing in a bathtub
out in the street?

naked of course
and the mouth of an octopus
between her legs. Puss surmounted
legs wrapt rapt around wound
around her thighs alive with the joy
that cometh in the morning

49

Post Enlightenment
we reach the Berlin dancefloor
or the beaches of Sydney
We no longer stand in a garden
under that now fake sun
Everything happens indoors
in the blue glow of the ordinateur
Warm colours (that old fashioned notion)
where is the new black?
And I can't even stand by the lies
folded double in snappy glasses with trademark frames

I have been prepared for the less dangerous
not for this . . .

50

it is a different kind of emptiness
to trust in background
tea stained wallpaper
the colour of leaves in the Fall

Adults make crayon drawings
yellow ties
and a little dog looks for warmth

I used to comfort myself
that the news gets out by cell phone
but the truth is
politicians still stand at podiums surrounded by flags

and the strong city may be destroyed

51

The surface of the moon
smooth where it has touched briny water
dips into the ocean
and is changed by the action of the waves

over the wharves
there are intervals developing in the sky
space and silence that opens

It may be just a distortion of hope
but I see moonlight
on the promised land

52

for ephemera here is a man
cast into the sea unfinished
sand still clinging to his legs
he is in a place I can't imagine
a place of danger
his glasses sit a little too high on his head
how could he see, how can he be found?
I was under sail to him
already stretching out my hand

in the morning light
happy to wake and see you

53

a pause between sets of waves

we float
on the water inside our heads
not seeing each other
aware only of ourselves

A twitch
from the muscles of the face
an eyelid's
neon blink
as a splash of firework words

. . . and the light of daylight streams in

54

light piles up in chandeliers
and metal grilles

icebergs that skid down the coast
more under the surface than above
water hardened and refracted
     —   what more of beauty?
arctic melt reorders sea-levels It is a love story
that defies a happy ending

An empty page
a snowfield of white paper

55

through the whole day a constant
at the bathhouse pummelled by water
I am gleaming, my slicked back hair
this cleanliness
this chilled baptismal torrent

(she leans over his bent back
composed
like a stem of an always-Mapplethorpe lily)

what is hidden?

a door that handles
the moment of entry

56

Who will walk through
those doors?
possess this over-exposed landscape
left naked in the glaring silence
between pale sky and snow?

Even when I hear nothing in response
from the top of the stairs
I see abandoned bicycles, music
and chilled wine
(technically you cannot see music)

the hand
of the god of made things now unmade

57

Under this distinct horizon
modernist architecture or the Brooklyn Bridge
Humans and deities
and everything else: the animals and birds
the nickel the dime the quarter
and whatever else
whoever else lies captive on the studio floor
all below unlikely beauty

Hold your breath the city tells me
everything is already mine
there is nothing that is not already mine

I will wake early—look through to the sky

58

owned, nothing—nothing nothing

intoxicating heady blasphemous
shameless knowing transgressive bliss
Forget the past this is the outskirts
of a prior conversation that obsesses
looking through her legs
at Thursday's unexpected moments
that anatomically don't add up
his/her spectacular curves reached on horseback
so nothing so mine. A man is a king
is a god confronted/confounded by this beauty

And a woman what is she?

59

on the outside nothing changes

There is a skinny dog with over large paws
a girl sitting on a step looking to one side
pearls to pinkly pedicure her feet
Out of overlooking windows
friends are talking heads unable to agree
Captivity has welded little yellow twist ties
to a hanging dream, a pencil stub on a shelf
an inheritance remembering the path of life
le plaisir est pour moi
the unlikeliest encounters redefine us
make being unexpectedly holy

60

a lightness I know sounds pathetic
but feels like walking on air
night is pierced with holes
and a cartel of laughter

It is vacation time the sidewalk is warm
enough reason to celebrate I decide
Family, friends, visitors to the city arrive
too soon furniture is balanced outdoors
in strange unnatural poses
so that all of us lean into each other

Unable to influence the buffet of sweet wet cakes
no one will ever leave

www.ingramcontent.com/pod-product-compliance
Lightning Source LLC
Chambersburg PA
CBHW031932080426
42734CB00007B/655